Blue Front

Other Books by Martha Collins

Poetry
Gone So Far (chapbook)
Some Things Words Can Do
A History of Small Life on a Windy Planet
The Arrangement of Space
The Catastrophe of Rainbows

Translation
Green Rice: Poems by Lam Thi My Da (with Thuy Dinh)
The Women Carry River Water: Poems by Nguyen Quang Thieu
(with the author)

Criticism
Critical Essays on Louise Bogan, editor

Blue Front

Martha Collins

Graywolf Press
Saint Paul, Minnesota

Publication of this volume is made possible in part by a grant provided by the Minnesota State Arts Board, through an appropriation by the Minnesota State Legislature; a grant from the Wells Fargo Foundation Minnesota; and a grant from the National Endowment for the Arts, which believes that a great nation deserves great art. Significant support has also been provided by the Bush Foundation; Target, with support from the Target Foundation; the McKnight Foundation; and other generous contributions from foundations, corporations, and individuals. To these organizations and individuals we offer our heartfelt thanks.

MINNESOTA
STATE ARTS BOARD

NATIONAL
ENDOWMENT
FOR THE ARTS

Published by Graywolf Press
2402 University Avenue, Suite 203
Saint Paul, Minnesota 55114
All rights reserved.

www.graywolfpress.org

Published in the United States of America

ISBN 1-55597-449-X

2   4   6   8   9   7   5   3   1
First Graywolf Printing, 2006

Library of Congress Control Number: 2005938152

Cover design: Kyle G. Hunter

in memory of William E. Collins (1904–1988)

in memory of Will "Froggie" James (1884?–1909)
as well as
Anna Pelley (1885?–1909) and Henry Salzner (1881?–1909)

and for Linda Lightfoot
without whom this book would not have been written

Blue Front

He was five. He sold
fruit on the street in front

He sold fruit. People came
He made change

came to see him
make change

———

in front of the restaurant that faced
the tracks that ran by the river
one of the rivers a block
from the street and up

to the double arch
where in 1909

was it the blue of the

was it the river

front of the blue of

———

the rivers make
a V where they meet
a point

the rivers flow
together but not
at once two

colors blue
and brown meet
make a line

———

Boats came from the north they came from the south

Trains came from the south they came from the north

Boats came on the blue Ohio they came on the brown Mississippi

Boats came on the brown they changed for the blue

Trains crossed that river people changed for the north the south

People changed in the middle of the river they changed cars

In the middle of the river they changed colors made a line

———

the street was Commercial

Dowling Pressing

Saloon   Drugstore   Opera House

Three States Buggy   Champion Tools

Dowling Pressing Club was where

his uncle's Blue Front Restaurant he was five

couldn't look out the same
window couldn't read
the same books laundry
couldn't be washed
in the same machines

I believe the institution
noble I believe it God's

water came from the same
source but couldn't be drunk
from the same fountains

couldn't be flushed

a town where people lived
together black and white

even there, where they changed
cars when they saw the invisible
line on that river saw it as clear
as the line between the two rivers

the failure of civil authorities
to maintain law and order makes

couldn't be washed

even sixty years later when a man
was found the same story hanged
the same town hanged but this
time hanged in the city jail but this

fountain filled with blood
that washes white

track

might have been from the other side but here
the other side was a river on both sides trains
ran if you started out on the wrong if
you fell off if you lost you might not cross
a visible line but nevertheless wherever
you were there were ways to find to put
for example dogs to follow a path beaten
by or as by an animal say a scent
to make to move quickly in order to stop
in his own who might not cover to stay
on the right no question of getting off to follow
into the house the fields the woods by whatever
means a horse a hijacked train some wagons
to follow the indisputable evidence down

yes there was also the other railroad the underground
railroad that ran on the water around the town around
the roads yes this was the place where Huck and Jim
should have changed rivers brown to blue yes this
was the land of Lincoln half a state from the village
where he the city where he the courts and the circuit
yes this was the north it meant freedom and there
were people no doubt in the town who yes of course

but there was also the other railroad the railroad talked
about even less the reverse underground railroad with
its bounty its tickets back to the south and it is also
true that further north in that city of Lincoln a year
before two others were also with even less reason they
had merely tried to protect their homes a failure of civil
order that caused a riot that led to the NAACP and moved
a woman Ida B. Wells-Barnett who meant to see that the law

where his cousin lived she was just his age they are back to back in a
studio portrait white bow in her hair circa 1909

where in 1908 a black was accused of killing a white another black of
raping a white

where the Lincoln home the Lincoln tomb the Lincoln depot the
Lincoln pew are tourist attractions monuments to the martyred
Illinois man who freed the slaves

where in 1908 a mob finding the prisoners gone burned the trans-
porting car destroyed 24 black businesses 40 black homes killed
2 successful blacks and also accidentally 4 whites

where he would later take his wife and child to visit the cousin the
Lincoln home the Lincoln tomb

where in 1908 events occurred that led a 1909 Cairo paper to say
its citizens *were not moved by race prejudice, nor did they permit themselves
to be led into wanton destruction of property, or the taking of innocent lives,
as in Springfield*

was five he was
my father he sold
fruit on the street

when I was five I
had a wagon went
to school in a checked

dress he had
a wagon a sailor
suit I had a checked

blanket for naps I had
not seen what he
had seen something

His friend was Margaret Rust.
She had a dog named Spot.
He had a wagon. They played.

———

on Commercial one block in
from Ohio six blocks up
the arch lit bright with lights

someone must have held
him up his uncle his father's
shoulders so he could see

———

A girl he could have known found the woman.
Later they could have gone to the same school.
She was three. Or she was seven. He was five.

———

Auntie Fay was his friend
a lady he said a lady

*her skin was black but her heart
was white* she wrote of herself

in the Testament she gave him she
was washed in the blood of the lamb

———

fourteen years later rode around town

dressed in a white sheet just

made noise he said made noise

clothes were washed baskets wooden
pins hung on lines strung from tree
to tree white for under white
for sleep sheets empty
sleeves above where heads

bread was baked grain corn
white and cakes his mother's
thirteen-egg-white angel

clothes were washed
cloths or was it clothes
with blood scrubbed

baskets napkins white
bread ribs and chicken
deviled eggs cakes for these
occasions celebrations often food

too late this time for baskets
not for liquor all saloons
stayed open in and out

and children tucked
into bed into white sheets

Birmingham

Because after I'd seen the church where it
was bombed where the four bodies were stacked
on top of each other said Josephine Marshall
Tuskegee '33 she saw nothing
but bloody sheets

    laundry couldn't be washed
    in the same machines

and read about this City of Churches this Magic
City this Bombingham where Shuttlesworth's
church and house had been bombed where Chambliss
before that Sunday had bombed homes for twenty
years where because of *Brown* the Klan castrated
a man who'd done nothing not even looked
at a white woman in '57

    couldn't read a book
    about black and white rabbits

because after I'd seen the two fountains the
replicated streetcar classroom courtroom the actual
door of that Birmingham Jail cell and followed
the tapes of the sit-ins the kneel-ins the marches
the students the children the hoses the dogs
and listened again to the famous speech

    couldn't be sworn in
    on the same Bible

the museum led to a hall they called it
Procession Hall where simply to walk was to join
the life-sized marchers because I had sat in a classroom
had only read the papers when it happened

Olive Branch

Horseshoe Lake

Turn on Promised Land Road
for Public Hunting

Future City

Welcome to Cairo

káy-roe not *ký-roe*
but once the queen

of this Little Egypt
these rivers its Nile

———

knew the Seventh Street house was gone
knew the Blue Front Restaurant was gone
forgot the downtown was almost closed down

nineteenth-century buildings that looked
like the buildings he knew like the Blue Front looked
except that except for a few there was nothing inside

———

ducks and geese
from Horseshoe Lake

from the rivers
catfish crawfish

———

14

no one walked or drove on Commercial
nothing was open except for a single store
a saloon and nothing was new except

at the Eighth Street intersection
where once two electric steel arches
had crossed in the center bright with lights

and now in the same center a clock
rising like a statue from a circular pedestal made
of donor-named bricks and draped with a chain

and on the street old-fashioned streetlamps
and one block up coming off the highway
a wrought-iron sign arching over the street

HISTORIC DOWNTOWN CAIRO

lived with his mother's Uncle Jim who owned
the Blue Front with Uncle Guy who was both uncle
and cousin her mother's uncle married her father's sister

Guy's Blue Front
Restaurant and Lunch Room
First Class Meals
Nicely Furnished Rooms
Travelers Lunches Put Up Day and Night
All the Delicacies of the Season

the uncles had come with their widowed mother
to Cairo Gate to the South and Southwest best shipping
facilities railway tonnage river tonnage five lines of railway

with tiled floors and tin ceilings
white tablecloths white napkins
in glasses wooden chairs stools
at the lunch counter one of 21
restaurants (10 white and 11
colored) and 7 newsstands

his father worked in the kitchen and he sold fruit in front
of the Blue Front four doors down from the depot
to travelers he was five he could make change

two weeks before it happened: President Taft

two years before: President Roosevelt

forty years before: President Grant

who had earlier come as General Grant to launch
the Union troops to the south that many residents
hoped would win having kin perhaps across one
of the rivers who had perhaps slaves postcards
of what occurred later were sent to Kentucky

near the end of the same century: President Clinton

who came when downtown was almost shut down
whose bus was surrounded by red white and blue
like the bunting the living flag of 600 children
surrounding President Taft whom thousands
came to town to see in October 1909

not to mention Dickens and Trollope and the TV
show Real People this was long after hundreds
or was it thousands came to make altogether
10,000 including children on parents' shoulders
who saw what occurred in November 1909

lynch

not as in pin, the kind that keeps the wheels
turning, and not the strip of land that marks
the border between two fields. unrelated
to link, as in chain, or by extension whatever
connects one part to another, and therefore
not a measure of chain, which in any
case is less than the span of a hand hold-
ing the reins, the rope, the hoe, or taking
something like justice into itself, as when
a captain turned judge and gave it his name.
that was before it lost its balance and crossed
the border, the massed body of undoers
claiming connection, relation, an intimate
right to the prized parts, to the body undone.

it is supposed that it is believed that Miss
Anna Pelley Miss Annie Pelley Miss Anne
Miss Pelly age 24 age 22 who worked

in the Pupkin Dry Good store and lived
an orphan who lived with her married sister

———

was five would not have seen he could
have known the little girl who found
the body she was seven or three but that
would not have been till the next day

———

it is known she left work at 6:00 P.M. took a streetcar
at 6:19 it is known she got off on Elm Street which was dark

it is known she carried an alligator bag some yards
of red goods to make a dress these items were not found

———

graduated from high school played
on the high school basketball team

———

it is supposed she was assaulted on Elm
near her home it is believed she struck

her assailant who gagged *with such*
cruel force it is thought he carried
her into the alley assisted

the ground showed she was dragged

it is known she was outraged *not a doubt*
and strangled *a virgin unquestionably pure*

this time there was a body it was a white
body murder it was a woman's body rape

———

said *him* because she was large and he
was larger he was large enough said
him because she was white and he
was black and could have therefore
must have necessarily him because

———

was what they said it always was was why they said
they had to must but it wasn't always rape (alleged) it wasn't
always murder (alleged) it wasn't always even alleged it

———

jumping a contract jilting
a girl introducing smallpox
being prosperous being insane

assaulting accusing testifying
against talking to white
men frightening children

coming to town remaining
in town being unpopular
being related to someone

being unrelated the wrong
person being someone one
of them had to be someone

bloodhounds got the scent
from the flour-sack cloth found
in the mouth led authorities

to Poplar Street then more
hounds more to the same place
and later all the way to the city jail

where Will 'Froggie' James
Will the Frog Will alias Frog
who drove for Cairo Ice and Coal

who stayed with Loving Green
who stayed with Georgia Cooper

———

to Poplar Street the house of Loving
Lovey Lovie Green *a negress of bad repute*
where James stayed she was found

washing no Georgia Cooper who lived
on 30th Street where James lived was found
washing a cloth that *exactly matches* no

a similar cloth no clothes no cloth was also
arrested no but Loving Green was arrested
Will James was arrested while driving his wagon

Will Thomas and Arthur Alexander
who lived with Green were also arrested

———

might have heard by
now his father his uncles
his mother would surely

have heard on the street
where he sold fruit in front
of the Blue Front would

have heard that they
had heard something

James was at Poplar Street he said
at 6:30 the time of the crime
Loving Green said 9:00

no scratches blood
no missing items

but Anna Pelley's sister said
he delivered ice last summer he
was *insolent* she had complained

------

meanwhile someone called to the crowd
and volunteered to lead some stepped forward
but many held back *Come on, boys!* and a mad rush

authorities are taking extraordinary precautions
to protect their prisoners because excitement
is high in all parts of Cairo

drag

a woman this time, to haul down the street, the alley,
before or after, with friction, resistance, but less
if the killer was large, like this one, could have, must
have, therefore not prolonged, like a story, but right
now, a trail, a scent, to pull or otherwise move
with force from the house, the shack, the barn,
the woods, the city or county jail, the one
who slowly, painfully, maybe in chains, the mob
itself, along by itself, moved into this, and this
one now, along the ground, down the street, up
to the place where, rope in their hands, to force
the truth, they said, and when it was done, down
the street to that alley, a mile away, this
one, now, its great weight, with great effort

rope, to bind body

strong rope, with noose

steel arch, provided by city

lighting, provided by arch

dry goods box (barrel?) for scaffold

clothesline rope, to attach to noose

bullets, to shoot into air and body

boards and other scavenged wood

coal oil, to ignite wood

knives, for removal of head and other

hitching post (tire stick?) for head

alcohol, as needed, before and during

Christmas was worst his father home late
from the Blue Front drunk saloons a bad
drunk his father the Christmas in 1909
the month after someone so he could see
his uncle his father's shoulders held
him late stayed open in and out and then
the Governor closed the saloons for five days

———

NO LOITERING, NO DRINKING ON THE STREET
(May 2001)

———

In 1904 the year he was born there were 50
saloons 24 on Commercial and on Ohio 7 one
The Owl on one side and one on the other

In 1909 there were 69 and 6 distributors 5
on Ohio where Little Egypt Handmade
5 cent Segars and Egypto Habana 10 cent

were made tobacco grew in Kentucky
across the river and there was also Lee
Hick Mail Order Liquor c/o The Owl Saloon

that was right next door on the north side
of the Blue Front Restaurant and on the south
side there was another there were plenty

———

Lohrs Standard Temperance Drinks
Royal Champagne Cider, Pure Birch Beer
Buffalo Mead, Standard Nerve Food

———

two years later his father would quit and never
his mother would join the WCTU they would leave
for another town where twelve years later he
would join the at least associate with the ride
around town with twelve years after his father
quit and never again they left that town for good

couldn't read the same books read only the others' old

couldn't be served in restaurants only backdoor take-out kitchens

couldn't swim in the swimming pool or skate at the skating rink

few could work in federal county city factories stores

laundry couldn't be washed in the same machines

———

in 1883 they marched they got their own high school in

1946 they sued got equal pay for teachers in

1953 they staged a protest got the movies in

1963 they got the swimming pool the skating rink but when

the pool was opened to all no whites would come it closed

Auntie Fay who didn't cook his
mother cooked for the uncle and aunt
they lived with who was Auntie Fay

Barnett who cooked for my mother's
family she had a son but she cooked
for my mother's just the same her

Cecil who cleaned for my mother
and prayed with my mother *if they
were all like Cecil* my father said

and none in their schools and only
one in my junior high and high
school there was always only one

he was seventeen he
wore a fake mustache
a white collar and tie
for the junior play

he waited outside
the school the church
for the girl he would later
marry she was also seventeen

———

was seventeen he
worked before and
after school he

opened and closed
the drugstore every
day he made change

———

would later take the train to Chicago
to go to pharmacy school he would

not finish the year he would come
back home and open and close

the store and later briefly probably
certainly not for long would join

in 1921 the *charming Margaret the young*
daughter of Mr. and Mrs. Rust was seen

wearing she later painted angels women
and children she never married was she

on that street in 1909 she lived
on Seventh Street where her friend

his parents his relatives lived a block
from Commercial Street where in 1909—

and where in 1883 some people
marched on their way to the high school

where she would graduate later teach
some *gray-headed bucks and wenches bowlegged*

unwashed pickaninnies came to the door
that was barred by the *brave girls* teaching

where she would teach and said (the book
says) *we'uns wants to gradiate like white*—

in 1921 the charming Margaret Rust a year
before she would graduate was seen wearing

a knickerbocker suit the town's first *decidedly*
attractive the paper said she died a year

before school integration she had a dog
named Spot a bow in her hair in 1909 before

November 10

mutterings of lynchings heard all day
would he have heard?

there may be a lynching tonight
in the High School Notes

———

at 7:00 P.M. the sheriff and deputy
boarded the train at Union Depot
four doors down from the Blue Front
where he sold fruit would he have seen

he wouldn't have seen the train
make an extra stop for the prisoner
who was *spirited away* from jail
and into the sheriff's hands

———

The train went north it was headed for Centralia

Word came of a mob at Anna the home of Anna Pelley

The sheriff deputy prisoner got off at Dongola before Anna

The livery stable had burned they couldn't get a rig or horses

They set off therefore asked for the road to Cypress

They took a wrong turn encountered a creek

Lost three times they walked all night in the woods

———

meanwhile at nine the mob went to the city
jail they searched the cells wooden and steel
struck matches threatened to lynch the police
chief and jailer if they would not produce

the mob was composed almost entirely of strangers

at ten they went to the county jail where Salzner
who murdered his wife was held then intercepted
the interurban streetcar and went to the jail
at Mound City and failed to find

FIFTEEN REAL PHOTO POSTCARDS Part One

1
Oval studio portrait, c. 1907
inscribed *Will James (alas) Froggie*
Gelatin silver print
Real photo postcard. 3½ x 5½

> *To familiarize our* New Studio *with the public*
> *and to secure a nice collection of Cairo faces*
> *we will sell 100 coupons good for sittings*

2
Home of Miss Anne Pelley
Gelatin silver print etc.

> *$3.00 Cabinet Oval $1.00*
> *$6.00 Cabinet Oval or Square $2.00*

3
Home of the seven-year-old Miss Boren
who found the body of Miss Pelley
LeBlock etched on negative

> *LEBLOCK'S STUDIOS*
> *209 Eighth Street*
> *BOTH PHONES OPEN EVENINGS*
> (Cairo Bulletin 11.14.09)

4
The Hounds
etched on negative
trains in background
four men with dogs
identified in ink on reverse

> *Sheriff Kolp. Charlston Mo*
> *Jailer Lutz. Cairo Ill*
> *Dupitt sheriff. Rilley of Williffee Ky*
> *Chief Egan. Of Cairo Ill*

5-9
include
the *course the hounds took*
the trains the mob took over

> Addressed (see also others)
> to *Mrs. Jake Petter, Paducah Ky*

to Cairo the first Union troops in the West in April 1861

to Cairo Ulysses S. Grant who knew the rivers would be strategic

to Cairo Fort Defiance 12,000 troops

to Cairo prostitutes liquor saloons a river town already destined

from Cairo to Fort Donelson Shiloh Vicksburg

to Cairo from Vicksburg 30,000 prisoners

from Cairo the most southern point in all the North

———

in 1898 *when black and white fought shoulder
to shoulder* said John J. Pershing troops
were stationed again in Cairo

———

*to maintain peace and order the Second Brigade
of the Illinois National Guard four companies
of the Fourth Regiment six altogether are now
in Cairo at 12:20 P.M.* on November 12 1909

*the presence of soldiers somewhat grotesque
a more peaceful community difficult to find
but we will enjoy entertaining as in
the Spanish-American War the gallant soldiers*

———

on July 15 1967 black soldier Robert L. Hunt
was hanged the same story hanged but this time hanged

in the city jail they called it a suicide they quickly
embalmed there were black protesters harsh

police on July 19 the National Guard to Cairo

hang

as a mirror on a wall, or the fall
of a dress. a dress, a shirt on a line
to fasten to dry. on the rack, or back
in the closet again, a sweet curse
on it all, sliver of nail, delayed
attack. shamed creature, a curse
on itself, so the act of doing it
changes the verb, tense with not
quite right. with rope, like a swing
from a tree. from a pole, like a flag,
or holidays, from an arch lit bright
with lights. in the night, in the air
like a shirt. without, or with only
a shirt. without, like an empty sleeve.

there was a second another
a white there were two
that night the second an after

thought said one of the papers
the other said when they couldn't find
the second black in the jail they took

instead the white who'd murdered
his wife because (she said before
she died) she'd refused—

not *prejudice* the papers
said *the hanging of Henry Salzner*
proves they were not moved by race

Montgomery

In the Dexter Avenue King Memorial Baptist Church where he found
his mission his voice

If you will protest courageously

the church that earlier met in a former slave traders pen the church
that was built with bricks discarded by workers paving the street

courageously and with Christian love

that was built a block from the State Capitol where 'it would not be
fitting or proper for colored people to build' beginning in 1883

when the history books are written

the church with a mural depicting events beginning in 1955 and
including Posey's Parking Lot where station wagons and cars picked
up people who did not would not ride the bus for thirteen months

written for future generations

to which one of the other visitors pointed and said 'That's where
we picked them up' so I knew he had been there and these were his
out-of-town friends

the historians will pause and say:

who graciously took me with them to the parsonage that was bombed

'There lived a great people—a black people—

and one of them said 'I hope you don't mind my asking but why
would a white person want'

who injected meaning and dignity into the veins of civilization.'

in 1967 when black citizens took to the streets to protest after
Robert L. Hunt was hanged or otherwise died in the city jail

> *they called the National Guard and formed the White Hats*

in 1968 just after the schools were fully integrated

> *they opened a school for whites called Camelot*

in 1969 when the United Front of Cairo began a boycott of stores
that wouldn't hire blacks and weekly marches

> *the White Hats allegedly fired into black housing*

in 1969 when reports disbanded the White Hats and courts defended
the marchers

> *firings violence gun battles clubbings increased*

in 1975 when after years of boycotts marches hearings the courts at
last ordered hirings

> *the white businesses rather than change closed down*

1828	20 *
1861	2,200 **
1870	6,267
1890	10,324
1900	12,566
1904	16,147 ***
1908	20,168 ***
1910	14,548
1920	15,203
1930	13,532
1960	9,348
1970	9,277
1980	5,931
2000	3,632

*   *estimate; black slaves, constructing buildings*
**   *estimate; also 12,000 Union troops*
***   *unofficial, from Cairo City Directory*

other figures based on U.S. Census

He was also five
once this Will this Frog perhaps
his name when he was ten
from play or friends or was
it later his voice

And he was seventeen
once too he could have gone
to school Sumner High
(colored) had been in town
since the 1883 protests

But we do not know
if he went to school
above average intelligence
says a 1910 book but adds
for one of his race

And we do not know
when he came to town the book
says *a number of years* but his name
is not in the directory which
would have listed him as *(col)*

He had a mother father he was born
in Tennessee his death certificate
says that is all we know except
he drove a wagon delivered
for Cairo Ice and Coal

He had his picture taken
mustache close-cropped hair
suspenders before they made
a postcard after before he stayed
with Loving Green and Georgia

Cooper if he had married
the town would have paid
by law $5,000 he had
no known heirs to collect
had no one to tell his story

prisoner sheriff in Belknap house awaiting the northbound train

in Karnac for food the sheriff saw Cairo conductor

to woods met strangers on horses men with guns

in woods saw Mr. Logan he knew from Cairo

in woods began to recognize crowd from Cairo

in woods surrounded by overpowered by crowd

back to house in Belknap now in flames *Burn him alive*

> *the crowd was composed*
> *almost entirely of strangers*

it was read in the Cairo paper the sheriff prisoner
left the train in Dongola the sheriff was seen
by a Cairo lumberman told the conductor telegraphed
Miss Pelley's brothers it was learned received
in the early afternoon the prisoner deputy
sheriff were seen near Karnac a town on the Big
Four railroad a crowd demanded hijacked took
possession a freight train with 300 men in cars
a gray-haired woman atop the caboose waving
her hands cheering arrived were informed of likely
direction followed shots brought others together
took possession at 5:00 P.M. threatened to burn
the prisoner women hissed and spit in Karnac sheriff
deputy prisoner 300 others caught the southbound train

a short, across, through neighbors' yards,
down alleys, under fences, in order to get
there, not to miss, to see or maybe even
participate, as if to redeem some slight
or grievous, recent or old, as if to repair
the oldest of all, the one that made us,
freed of that water, breathers of air,
bearers of darkness, incomplete, in need
of another, eye to see, ear to hear,
to save in a jar, a drawer, off, a body
claimed, partaken of, ours, and later
down, if the body held, from bridge
or tree or arch, loose, removed from us
by us, expunged, end of scene, away

he was ten
he worked before
and after he opened

and closed before
and after school
he swept he stocked

the shelves he waited
in the drugstore
he made change

———

his father's father had supervised
in that mining town where he worked on Main

but since they left the river town
his father had worked in the Paradise Mine

(his father's father disappeared? died?)
his father had joined the union

———

his mother joined
the WCTU, the Eastern
Star, the Christian Church

she'd taught school she
kept her books in that tiny
house there were books

his father's father owned a mine

   supervised a mine

his mother's father's ancestor signed the Constitution
governed Pennsylvania had his portrait painted by Copley

   his mother's father came in the nineteenth century

all his family except the Swiss who went to Cairo were English

   came in the nineteenth century from Ireland

There were trees on those streets that were named
for trees: Sycamore, Cedar, Poplar, Pine,
Elm, where the woman's body was found,
where the man's body was taken and burned—

There must have been trees, there were trees
on Seventh Street, in front of the house that stands
in the picture behind the carriage that holds
the boy's mother, the boy's cousin, the boy—

And of course there were trees on Washington
Avenue, wide boulevard lined with *exotic*
ginkgoes, stately magnolias, there were trees
on that street that are still on that street,

trees that shaded the fenced-in yards of the large
Victorian houses, the mansion built by the man
who sold flour to Grant for the Union troops,
trees that were known to the crowd that saw

the victim hanged, though not on a tree, this
was not the country, they used a steel arch
with electric lights, and later a lamppost, this
was a modern event, the trees were not involved.

a crowd waited at Union Depot four
doors down from the Blue Front where

      would he have been there seen

but the train had stopped at Tenth the prisoner
dragged to Eighth and Commercial a rope

      would his father and uncle
      have carried him joined

men women and children *filled from side
to side the entire width of the 100-foot street
a wild rush* flashes of gunfire shouts

      would he have understood
      as they neared the arch

10,000 people massed together including
prominent citizens said a Chicago paper
another paper said led by citizens' wives

      and would his mother

a *great angry wave of humanity* shouted
'You dog! You black brute! Kill him! Burn him!'

      would he have understood

most of the few who could hear agreed
that James confessed said Alexander

      would he have seen he would

when someone turned on the lights on the arch
flooding the street the victim the crowd

he could have clearly seen

when they raised the victim so all could see
when someone lowered a rope and attached
when the rope was pulled by a dozen hands
said a Cairo paper Chicago said pulled
by Miss Pelley's sister / her female relatives
aided by scores of / 500 screaming women

he would have seen

when the rope broke and the living body fell

he would have seen

when they dragged the victim fifty feet
shot 500 bullets into him dragged him heavy
to throw to the river but changed their minds

and maybe that was all would not
have seen it was twenty blocks
away his father mother so late

when they rushed to the scene of the first crime
where a woman lit the fire a Chicago paper
said while the crowd *danced and shrieked*
(a Cairo paper said *quiet and earnest*)

and while the body was burning they cut
off the half-burnt head cut open the chest cut
out the heart for souvenirs someone cut off
a foot *a great prize* and later some bits of bone

and placed the half-burnt head in a park
on a hitching post / a tire stick / a pole

and then found Henry Salzner a few blocks away
in the county jail would anyone even have mentioned

a white man he didn't say

burn

a slow. to feel pain as if or from:
his face in the wind. to give off light
or glow: the electric arch. to produce
a stinging: whiskey in their throats.
to feel what they said he felt or they
with rage. for warmth or food: wood,
fuel. a slow. scorch blacken char:
the roast the body. in another place,
the barbecue we had. the body lowered,
lifted, lowered. a slow. the feet
the calves a knee: ash in the air. here
whiskey, the wind. damned consumed.
always desire. the question. offering of.
cinders, bones. charred head on a post.

he was five would surely
not have seen when they took

the second the white from jail
it was nearly midnight far

from home and later he mentioned
only the one on Commercial

———

sledge hammer for steel cell door

stronger rope than used for first

telephone pole, provided by city

3 bullets for body, others for air

knives for cutting face and rope

———

but this time let the victim
pray *services for his soul* with *bowed
and uncovered heads* a *disciplined*

crowd fetched rope and climbed
the pole there were bullets and knives
but only rope for souvenirs

FIFTEEN REAL PHOTO POSTCARDS Part Two

10
Scene at Hustler's Arch
Night of November 11, 1909
LeBlock etched on negative

> *Pictures of the lynching have appeared in the city,*
> *the lighted arch and sea of people under it standing out well.*
> *The negro cannot be seen in the picture.*

11
Half Burned Head of James
etched on pole on negative
houses in background
LeBlock etched on roof

> *Another picture is that of the skull as it looked*
> *when impaled on the tire stick and placed in the park.*
> (Cairo Bulletin, 11.14.1909)

12
Ashes of James
X and *LeBlock* also etched
seven boys white and black
on two sides of ashes with coal oil tins
inscribed in ink on reverse

> *the cross is where Miss Pelley was found*

13

TELEPHONE POLE ON WHICH

HENRY SALZNER, WAS

HANGED NOV 11TH 1909

FOR MURDERING HIS WIFE

six men five in coats and hats

> *Salzner, a white man and photographer by trade*
> (Du Quoin Evening Call 11.12.09)

14

SPOT WHERE WILL JAMES, BODY

WAS RIDDLED WITH BULLETS, AFTER

BEING LYNCHED NOV 11TH 09

four men three women on street

with sign *Dowling Pressing Club Both Phones*

> May 27, 1908 amendment
> to US Postal Laws and Regulations
> forbids mailing of *matter of a character*
> *tending to incite arson, murder, or assassination*

15

Composite photo

with oval portrait in center

WILL JAMES, ALIAS FROGGE

Silver gelatin print

Real photo postcard 3 ½ x 5 ½

> addressed (see also others)
> to *Mrs. Jake Petter, Paducah Ky*

to kill. to more than kill. to kill again
and again and again. to send forth bullets
as buds from trees, from earth. the word
appeared before the gun, and even now
an arrow would do, but one by one as buds,
so many until. as blades of grass, fast,
as questions at, a growing child. up,
out, through: a bright thread. one
quick glance, another, the sudden guns.
off, out, down: the body filled. now
the camera aimed: the body again. rolls
of film: the crowd, the site, the scene.
the body again, the captured head on film.
how many bullets in it? go ahead, tell.

Often they cut off parts for souvenirs.

This time they cut out the heart they sliced it up.

Sometimes they cut off fingers they cut off toes.

They cut off other parts to cut them off.

Once they made the victim eat those parts.

Made him take them eat them made him chew.

Tell us you like it they said as they watched him eat.

Once they used giant corkscrews to bore the flesh.

Thus they raped the belly the chest the thigh.

Thus they made the infamous parts their own.

Thus like an X-rated movie they enjoyed.

And why this X-rated writing should it be read.

Children were often there they were being taught.

in 1924 fourteen years later or fifteen years later three
or four after the junior play the girl he would marry
away at school and he back home from school in the town
where he'd worked in the drugstore since he was ten

he waited he made change

where they must have come in their white robes and white
hoods and maybe they came to the Christian Church where
he'd joined the Christian Endeavor and maybe they marched
up the aisle with a contribution and note applauding

his mother joined

the Church's *efforts and great work* as they had in Williamson
County two counties over opposing mostly not blacks though they
of course were strictly white but bootleggers immigrants Catholics
mostly Italians who'd come for the mines and made and sold wine

his father never again

and although they took over Williamson County not to mention
the state of Indiana and much of the South where the lynchings
continued and sometimes increased it was after all after *The Birth
of a Nation* in 1915 that it rose for the first time since Reconstruction

noise he said made noise

it is probably true that for him in 1924 it wasn't just blacks
but someone anyone different or maybe just something to do
to join he paid his ten dollars and maybe attended barbecues
dances three-day Klantaquas or Klan Konclaves or maybe

rode around town

just motor parades with maybe a flaming cross on behalf
of white Gentile American manhood free public schools not
parochial law and order protection of womanhood constitution
prohibition rode around town dressed he said in a white sheet

Cairo today at the mercy of the mob

Several hundred soldiers ten regiments

1,500 would he have been there seen

Arthur Alexander named by James taken to jail

Removed to special train by soldiers with guns and bayonets

A gray-haired woman shouted *Will you see a black demon escape?*

A roar the crowd surged forward soldiers pushed back

A quiet day in the streets the usual business

Yesterday *no thievery pillaging no one injured except*

The coroner's jury report: *from the hands of parties unknown*

Most expressed pride *a good purpose a job well done*

A more peaceful community difficult to find

CAIRO REDEEMS HERSELF
(Belleville Illinois *News Democrat,*
November 12, 1909)

In ferociously dramatic fashion the infuriated populace staged a tragedy.

DEFIANCE THEATRE
4TH AND WASHINGTON
REVIVAL OF THE LEGITIMATE DRAMA
OF HAMLET PRINCE OF DENMARK
(1894 FLYER SEEN IN MAGNOLIA MANOR, CAIRO, 2001)

*The pent-up fountains of human passion, human resentment, and human
revenge broke forth.*

O, from this time forth,
My thoughts be bloody, or be nothing worth!
(*Hamlet* IV, iv)

*That punishment is most effective which follows quickly. A so-called mob out-
break is as much a magnificent and grand natural phenomena as a cyclone or
an earthquake, or a thunderbolt or a flood is, and it is much more unerring,
more just, and more terrible.*

Till the foul crimes done in my days of nature
Are burnt and purged away.
(*Hamlet* I, v)

*The militia is the farcical end of this superb tragedy drama. The curtain has
dropped on that play. The band has ceased to play, the crowd is gone, the
lights are out, the house is dark and it is over. The outburst has done its work
of purifying and of cleansing, and in that way it has fully accomplished its
heaven-destined purpose.*

Eleven white churches

Eleven black churches

Eleven white churches were thronged
with listeners all except
the Methodists heard

the failure of civil authorities
to maintain law and order
(Episcopal)

the lynchings it seems were necessary
to arouse the people to startle
(Presbyterian)

the worst class of criminal
is the criminal negro, the worst
creature on earth, the politician
has patted this class on the head as one
pats a dog but you would not pat a mad
dog with your hand, you would use a club
(Baptist)

But *Were the negroes given an environment*
that would lift them up, or were they encouraged
to live like dogs in miserable shanties, to pay
big rents and work for low wages?
(Episcopal)

The papers did not record
what was said in eleven black churches

But the 1968 minister of the same
Baptist Church clubbed a 73-year-old
black man to death for attempting
the minister said to rape his wife

A coroner's jury cleared the minister
who eight months later organized
in response to forced integration
the private school called Camelot

and who in 2003 was still minister
citizen leader whose church
in May 2001 proclaimed

Keep your day bright
by thinking right

sheets napkins bleached bread keep
your day bright by thinking pure
thought no body in it back before
bodies mouths and after all is clean
again fountains washed as snow brides
before or angels out of time who have
no bodies under if a lie intended not
to mean without words or print making
no mistake must be kept clean but color
crept into their cheeks were never free
from absent could be seen as blanched
deficient weakly colored bloodless blank
needing contrast to be seen at all against

He was forty. It was time
to buy a house. They bought

a nice house, with nice
yards, front and back, yards

where there were trees, ash
and elm, lots of shade.

———

the schools were white the church was white
the neighborhood of course was white he
owned his own pharmacy his customers
were also white till later when he worked
for someone else and said *if they were all*
but even then the rage beneath the smile
the secret alcohol were also white against
whom like his friends were white his daughter's
friends would also like her teachers all be white

———

later he would teach
his daughter to say
may I help you please

Ida B. Wells-Barnett

who had raised her younger siblings taught
then fought her removal from whites-only
sued the railroad won and started to write

who had agitated lectured in England
published pamphlets lynching cases numbers
challenged the usual arguments the WCTU

who moved to Chicago married had four children
ages five through ten the oldest told her to go
to Cairo because there was no one else

who went because she meant to see that the law
of 1905 which dismissed a sheriff who did
not do all to prevent a lynching was enforced

who convinced Cairo blacks who supported
the sheriff who hired black deputies that
the law must be enforced to prevent further

who argued the case in Springfield convinced
the governor won the praise of opposing
lawyers the sheriff would not be reinstated

who wrote of James as innocent since she knew
how *Black Rapes White* was used and showed
how often not and often consent and never *White* . . .

who would not have found the report of confession
before the hanging convincing *the mob invariably
reports the falsehood* she wrote in 1895

and while there were dogs and the problem of when
he was where or whether as some said later a white
man did it hired James to carry the body thus the scent

what mattered was that another had been presumed
guilty no question of proving she said who wrote
who offered The Remedy: *Tell the world the facts.*

Arthur Alexander was lynched in Anna the town where Anna Pelley was raised a town where *people do not like negroes and will not let them reside* in November 1909.

Not true.

Arthur Alexander would have been lynched in Cairo if he had not been removed by soldiers in November 1909.

Probably true.

John Pratt a convicted black purse snatcher would have been lynched in Cairo if the sheriff had not confronted a mob in February 1910.

Probably true.

Robert L. Hunt a black soldier found dead in the Cairo police station had hanged himself a suicide in July 1967.

Probably not.

and the soldiers became the soldiers
and the mob became the citizens
and the victim became a teenaged boy
who took the train from Chicago

and the mob became the soldiers
and the victim became the enemy
and the victim became the citizens
of another the enemy's country

bury

remains to rest in the beautiful sacred ground
a single white girl a white man killed by a mob
they came from the same town the same earth
all in the earth unless in a tomb at sea
or river they thought for the other but chose the air
a fire it was called a funeral pyre and what
could the undertaker take but bits of bone
ashes a half-burned head to put under ground
or in the dump the paper said but it named
the undertaker no heirs but perhaps some face
in some hands or someone lost at least in thought
while the mob consigned the infamous night itself
to oblivion, bone of a dog, garbage, concealed
beneath a mountain of words but not forgotten

he was twenty-three he
went again to pharmacy

school he took the train
to Texas he went south

he was twenty-four he
married finished school

in Texas liked Texas they
liked the space the open sky

but traveled back they had
a child he had an heir he

opened closed his own
store he worked he lived

a long life with some success
some common disappointments

what he had seen
is also what I was
I had to know

white what white
had done thought
what white does not

think an absence
white is not a given
point extended line

blank for signing *if*
you don't mind
my asking why

a white person
had to see my name
listed white *(wht)*

an other owing
what it is to what
it thinks it isn't

Selma

Although when I asked in Selma for the walking
tour brochure I was given the windshield tour
instead with 115 beautiful landmarks
and homes many pre-dating the burning
of this arsenal city in 1865—
                         and although
it seemed an afterthought that I finally got the small
brochure for the walking tour that passes Brown's
Chapel AME Church where thousands gathered
in 1965—
               still, I found Brown's where King
spoke when Jimmy Lee Jackson was killed
and a sign said *racism killed our brother* and nine
days later they gathered once again for the first
big march—
                 and the Voting Rights Museum
which held the shoes of the marchers the footprints
of the marchers in plaster the voter registration
lists the photographs taken for *Life*—
                    and through
the museum's window the Edmund Pettus Bridge
where first 600 then 1,500 then 4,000 left for Montgomery
where 25,000 finally marched to the capitol after
the nation took notice and LBJ said *We shall
overcome* and King said:
                 *Not long, because the arc
of the moral universe is long, but it bends toward justice.*

Two boys riding bikes on the levee,
  two girls together in front of a house,
    two women talking across a fence,
  one black, one white, in the library, city hall—

on Commercial a new restaurant, a few
  parked cars, a beauty salon, *Antiques,*
    and on Ohio, high on stilts, another
  restaurant overlooking the river—

and south of town, just south of the bridges,
  Fort Defiance Park, *SAVED IN 1987,*
    with a pavilion, picnic tables, swings,
  and the Boatmen's Memorial, shaped like a prow,

with steps to climb to view the confluence,
  a visible line, not quite straight, where blue
    and brown, with waters from 25 states,
  come together become a single flowing body—

He wanted to know
everyone in the end
he was a kind

man did errands
for old people younger
than he helped kids

with school met people
in stores on the street
please may I help

And the last day
he said *You know
this world could be*

*a better place just
promise me that you
will help* he waited

he made change may
I help you please
make change

There was the blue and there was the brown
or was it the greenish the milky white
there was the olive green the yellow
said Edna Ferber writing Showboat there
were showboats before there was town

There was the placid La Belle Ohio there
was the mighty Mississippi father of waters
they came together but often one or the other
flooded before and even after the levees
that kept and hid them from the town

But standing in front of the Blue Front
he could see the blue Ohio keelboats flatboats
lights on the barges at night he could hear
the whistles of steamboats the splashing
of paddlewheels lapping of water

There is the blue and there is the brown the rivers
flow together but not at once two colors meet
make a point of land a line that sometimes
wavers but still a line that we can cross
or not disappearing beyond the point

ACKNOWLEDGMENTS

I am deeply grateful to the Lannan Foundation for a residency grant in Marfa, Texas, where a substantial portion of this work was completed; to the Witter Bynner Foundation and the Santa Fe Art Institute for a residency grant during which it was begun; to the Santa Fe Art Institute for a second residency two years later; and to the Heinrich Böll Committee for a residency in Achill, Ireland, where final revisions were made.

Blue Front would not exist without the inspiration of Linda Lightfoot, whose conversation led me to Birmingham, Montgomery, and Selma, and thus to the beginning of the journey that finally became the book.

The Montgomery section is indebted and dedicated to Farrell, Roger, Winston, Michael, Arthur, and Dwight.

Without Sanctuary: Lynching Photography in America, the exhibit of postcards collected by James Allen which I saw in New York and which was the basis for the book of the same title (2000), led me back to Cairo. My deepest thanks to Myra Goldberg, who first told me about the exhibit, and to Allen, the first person I contacted about the Cairo lynchings. The two "postcard" sections of this book describe postcards featured in *Without Sanctuary* and quote from Allen's commentary.

Kathryn B. Ward, whose forthcoming book is essential reading for anyone interested in Cairo, has been a constant source of information and encouragement. The 1913–1964 section is based almost exclusively on her research, as is the supposition in the penultimate stanza of the Ida B. Wells-Barnett section; other sections draw on her work as well. Kathy's generosity and warmth have been invaluable.

Stacy Pratt McDermott's "An Outrageous Proceeding: A Northern Lynching and the Enforcement of Anti-Lynching Legislation in Illinois, 1905–1910," *Journal of Negro History* 84:16 (1999), 61–77, gave me my first detailed account of the Cairo lynchings and their aftermath. My thanks to her for directing me to this article.

In Cairo, Monica Smith has been wonderfully generous in allowing me to examine materials in the Cairo Public Library, including city directories and other historical materials, and in giving me a sense of present-day Cairo. I am immensely grateful for her assistance and hospitality.

I am also grateful to Preston Ewing, Jr., for conversations about Cairo's African-American history. Ewing's photographs, as well as the commentary and oral history edited by Jan Peterson Roddy, in *Let My People Go: Cairo, Illinois, 1967–1973* (1996), were a primary source of information about the period they document.

Exhibits in Cairo's U.S. Custom House Museum contributed to the sections beginning "Christmas was worst" and "in 1921 *the charming Margaret*" and provided information about Edna Ferber's visits to Cairo. In addition to the Museum, the "The Historic Cairo Illinois Website" (no longer online) provided useful background information, especially for the section beginning "two weeks before it happened."

I am centrally grateful to my father, William E. Collins, who told me about his early life and left me the results of research on his family as well as the Cairo of his childhood. I am also grateful to my mother, Katheryn E. Collins, who preserved postcards and photographs in a scrapbook documenting my father's life as well as her own.

My primary sources of information about the Cairo lynchings themselves were the following newspapers: *Cairo Bulletin, Cairo Evening Citizen, Chicago Daily News, Chicago Evening Post, Chicago Record-Herald, Chicago Tribune,* and *Du Quoin Evening Call*, the southern Illinois newspaper published by my maternal grandfather, Augustus W. Essick. I am grateful to the Illinois State Historical Library in Springfield for allowing me to photocopy all the relevant sections of these newspapers, which are cited frequently throughout this book. While I have not been thoroughly consistent in italicizing language taken from the newspapers, my general rule has been to italicize any passage longer than a few words, as well as language of any length that is clearly interpretive. All statements presented as factual are based on newspaper and other accounts.

Other sources include but are not limited to the following:

On historical Cairo: John M. Lansden, *A History of the City of Cairo Illinois* (1910, reissued 1976), which is cited in the section beginning "He was also five"; *History of Alexander, Union and Pulaski Counties, Illinois,* ed. William Henry Perrin (1883), which is the source of the 1883 information cited in the section beginning "in 1921 *the charming Margaret*"; promotional booklets and brochures, including *The Attractions of Cairo, Illinois* (1890) and *Cairo Illinois and Its Many Attractions* (1909), cited in the section beginning "lived with his mother's Uncle Jim" and elsewhere; and Cairo City Directories for 1900, 1904, and 1908–9, cited throughout.

On lynching: Numerous sources, including Walter White's *Rope and Faggot: A Biography of Judge Lynch* (1929), which is the primary source for the final part of the section beginning "this time there was a body"; James R. McGovern, *Anatomy of a Lynching: The Killing of Claude Neal* (1982), to which the section beginning "Often they cut" is indebted; Philip Dray, *At the Hands of Persons Unknown: The Lynching of Black America* (2002); and Trudier Harris, *Exorcising Blackness: Historical and Literary Lynching and Burning Rituals* (1984).

On responses to lynching, including the founding of the NAACP: Works by and about Ida B. Wells-Barnett, especially *Crusade for Justice: The Autobiography of Ida B. Wells,* ed. Alfreda M. Duster (1970) and *Southern Horrors and Other Writings: The Anti-Lynching Campaign of Ida B. Wells, 1892–1900* (1996). The quote at the end of the Ida B. Wells-Barnett section is from the latter collection. Issues of *The Crisis*, the NAACP publication begun in 1910, have also been useful.

On other cities, as well as Cairo: Travel and museum brochures, and occasionally websites. On Springfield: Roberta Senechal, *The Sociogenesis of a Race Riot: Springfield, Illinois, in 1908* (1990). On Birmingham: Diane McWhorter, *Carry Me Home: Birmingham, Alabama: The Climactic Battle of the Civil Rights Revolution* (2001).

On the Ku Klux Klan: Several works, especially those that focus on the rise of the Klan in the Midwest—Paul M. Angle, *Bloody Williamson: A Chapter in American Lawlessness* (1969); Richard K. Tucker, *The Dragon and the Cross: The Rise and Fall of the Ku Klux Klan in Middle America* (1991); and Leonard J. Moore, *Citizen Klansmen: The Ku Klux Klan in Indiana, 1921–1928* (1991).

On the Civil Rights Movement: Various sources, including museums, city and museum brochures, and Juan Williams, *Eyes on the Prize: America's Civil Rights Years, 1954–1965* (1987), which is the primary source for the first half of the section beginning "couldn't look out the same."

Finally, my thanks to *Ploughshares, Kenyon Review,* and *Michigan Quarterly Review,* which published selections from this book; to the William Joiner Center for the Study of War and Social Consequences, which gave me a supportive audience for public readings from it; and to Ted Space, who not only supported but also encouraged my immersion in it.

Martha Collins is the author of four collections of poetry, including *Some Things Words Can Do*, and co-translator of two volumes of poetry from the Vietnamese. Her awards include fellowships from the National Endowment for the Arts, the Bunting Institute, the Ingram Merrill Foundation, and the Witter Bynner Foundation, as well as three Pushcart Prizes and a Lannan Residency grant. Collins is Pauline Delaney Professor of Creative Writing at Oberlin College and lives in Oberlin, Ohio, and Cambridge, Massachusetts.

This book was designed by Rachel Holscher, set in Perpetua by Prism Publishing Center, and manufactured by Bang Printing on acid-free paper.